GRAPHIC PREHISTORIC ANIMALS

DAWN HORSE

EOHIPPUS

ILLUSTRATED BY ALESSANDRO POLUZZI

A+

Smart Apple Media

Published by Smart Apple Media, an imprint of Black Rabbit Books
P.O. Box 3263, Mankato, Minnesota 56002
www.blackrabbitbooks.com

Produced by David West ⚇ Children's Books
6 Princeton Court, 55 Felsham Road, London SW15 1AZ

Designed and written by Gary Jeffrey

Library of Congress Cataloging-in-Publication Data

Names: Jeffrey, Gary, author. | Poluzzi, Alessandro, illustrator.
Title: Dawn horse / written by Gary Jeffrey ; illustrated by Alessandro Poluzzi.
Description: Mankato, Minnesota : Smart Apple Media, an imprint of Black
    Rabbit Books, [2017] | Series: Graphic prehistoric animals | Audience: K
    to grade 3._ | Includes index.
Identifiers: LCCN 2015036964| ISBN 9781625884077 (library binding) | ISBN 9781625884237 (ebook)
Subjects: LCSH: Hyracotherium–Juvenile literature. | Hyracotherium–Comic
    books, strips, etc. | Horses, Fossil–Juvenile literature. | Horses,
    Fossil–Comic books, strips, etc. | CYAC: Horses, Fossil. | Prehistoric
    animals. | Horse family (Mammals) | LCGFT: Graphic novels.
Classification: LCC QE882.U6 W47 2017 | DDC 569.665/5–dc23
LC record available at http://lccn.loc.gov/2015036964

Printed in China
CPSIA compliance information: DWCB16CP
010116

9 8 7 6 5 4 3 2 1

CONTENTS

WHAT IS A DAWN HORSE?

EOHIPPUS MEANS "EARLY HORSE"

Eohippus lived around 55 million to 50 million years ago, during the **Eocene period. Fossils** of its skeleton have been found in North America and Europe (see page 22).

It is also called *Hyracotherium* which means "hyrax-like" because its fossil teeth looked like the teeth of a hyrax—a jungle rodent.

It had four hoofed toes on each front foot and three hoofed toes on each back foot.

It was the size of a modern-day fox.

It ate leaves and shoots.

EOHIPPUS MEASURED 24 INCHES (61 CM) LONG AND 14 INCHES (36 CM) HIGH. IT WEIGHED 55 POUNDS (25 KG).

Its small size and multi-toed feet stopped it from sinking into the boggy ground of the forest floor.

It had a large brain for its body size, meaning it was alert and intelligent.

This would be *Eohippus* and you.

Ten million years after the extinction of the dinosaurs, the world was very warm. Sub-tropical forests grew at the North and South Poles, while wet tropical rainforest covered North America and Europe. Many types of small, light mammals evolved to live in the steaming, swampy, overgrown jungles. Among them was a small, extremely agile, and alert **browser** with hooved feet called *Eohippus*.

Eohippus *had teeth designed for browsing—picking fresh leaves and new shoots.*

During the Eocene, there were two groups of hooved animals called **ungulates**. One group had an odd number of back toes. The other had an even number. In the Eocene, odd-toed ungulates, such as *Eohippuses* and tapirs, succeeded better than even-toed ungulates, such as mousedeer. *Eohippus*'s largest toe evolved into the single hoof of today's horse.

Grasslands had not yet appeared. These first horses had no plains and no herds. *Eohippus* had only its own wits and dense undergrowth to protect it, just like modern-day muntjac deer (below).

DAWN HORSE IN THE TROPICAL FOREST OF NORTH AMERICA

HIGH UP IN THE CANOPY OF A TROPICAL RAINFOREST IN THE AMERICAN MIDWEST, 50 MILLION YEARS AGO.

A SHOSHONIUS LEAPS FORWARD TO GRAB A BUG. IT WILL BE ITS LAST MEAL BEFORE THE DAWN BREAKS.

FAR BELOW, A HEAVILY PREGNANT EOHIPPUS PICKS HER WAY THROUGH THE DAMP FOREST FLOOR LOOKING FOR A DRY AND **SECLUDED** SPOT.

IT LOOKS AROUND ANXIOUSLY FOR PREDATORS. IT CAN WAIT NO LONGER. IT KNOWS IT MUST GIVE BIRTH.

BUT FROM DEEP WITHIN THE MASS OF BRANCHES, IT IS BEING WATCHED BY CATLIKE EYES.

THE EOHIPPUS CIRCLES AROUND A DRY PATCH OF MOSS. IT KEEPS A CAREFUL LOOKOUT FOR DANGER AND LIES DOWN TO WAIT.

JUST TWENTY MINUTES LATER, ITS NEWBORN FOAL HAS ARRIVED.

THE EOHIPPUS CLEANS THE FOAL AND NUDGES IT TO STAND UP.

THIS IS THE MOST DANGEROUS TIME. INSTINCTIVELY THE FOAL WOBBLES TO ITS FEET, HUNGRY FOR ITS MOTHER'S MILK.

JUST THEN A CATLIKE MACHAEROIDES BURSTS THROUGH THE UNDERGROWTH.

IT IS A SABERTOOTH!

GROWWL

THE MACHAEROIDES APPROACHES QUICKLY. THE BABY EOHIPPUS HAS TO LEARN TO RUN BEFORE IT CAN FEED.

THE MOTHER NIMBLY LEADS ITS FOAL THROUGH THE INTERTWINED VINE BRANCHES OF A HEAVY THICKET, WHICH BAR THE MACHAEROIDES'S WAY.

NESTLED IN THE SAFETY OF THE DEEP JUNGLE, THE FOAL CAN FEED AT LAST.

A FEW WEEKS LATER, THE EOHIPPUS FOAL IS NEARLY WEANED AND FOLLOWS ITS MOTHER TO AN AREA OF SPROUTING SHRUBS. OTHER *BROWSERS*, THE TAPIRLIKE HEPTODON AND ANCIENT MOUSEDEER, HAVE GATHERED HERE TO FEED.

AS THE EOHIPPUS FOAL *TENTATIVELY* SNIFFS AND LICKS AT THE SHRUBS' SHOOTS, A SHADOW PASSES OVER IT.

IT IS A GASTORNIS—A MIGHTY FLIGHTLESS BIRD WITH A MASSIVE BEAK. THE BROWSERS SCATTER AS GASTORNIS PLUNGES ITS HUGE FEET HEAVILY INTO THE MUD.

GRAAARRK!

GWHEEEE
GWHEEEE

THE GASTORNIS COCKS ITS HEAD. ITS BEADY EYES SEEM TO BE SEARCHING FOR SOMETHING.

BELOW, THE EOHIPPUS FOAL DARTS ABOUT IN CONFUSED PANIC. ITS MOTHER HAS GONE!

THE GASTORNIS SWOOPS DOWN TOWARD THE TERRIFIED EOHIPPUS...

GRAARK

...AND PLUNGES ITS BEAK DEEP INTO A LARGE *FIBROUS* FRUIT.

KRUNCH

WHILE THE GASTORNIS RIPS OUT AND CRUNCHES THE FRUIT'S SEEDS, THE EOHIPPUS DARTS OFF TO LOOK FOR ITS MOTHER.

POISED IN THE BRANCHES ABOVE, A TREE-CLIMBING OXYAENA LAUNCHES ITSELF DOWNWARD...

HSSSSSAGH

...AND CATCHES A SMALL NOTHARCTUS THAT HAD BEEN EATING NECTAR FROM A PLANT.

IN A DRIER PART OF THE FOREST, A WOLFLIKE MESONYX BUSILY GROOMS ITS MATE IN FRONT OF THEIR DEN.

SUDDENLY ITS EARS PRICK UP. WITHIN THE USUAL BIRD SCREECHES AND INSECT NOISES OF THE FOREST, IT CAN HEAR A SERIES OF FAINT CRIES.

IT RECOGNIZES THE SOUND OF A YOUNG DAWN HORSE—AN EASY AND TASTY MEAL. THE MESONYX SETS OFF TO FIND IT. ITS MATE FOLLOWS, AND THEY PASS UNDER A GROUP OF LEMURLIKE SMILODECTES THAT ARE FEEDING ON SAP FROM THE TRUNK OF A GUM TREE.

THE EOHIPPUS FOAL CRIES OUT. IT IS LOST AND AFRAID.

WHEEEHEEE

THE MESONYXES RUN SWIFTLY THROUGH THE BUSH ON THE TIPS OF THEIR HOOVED TOES, HEADING TOWARD THE SOUNDS OF THE FOAL.

ALTHOUGH AFRAID, THE EOHIPPUS IS ALSO VERY HUNGRY. IT MOVES TOWARD SOME TASTY-LOOKING SHRUBS NEAR THE EDGE OF A SWAMP.

BEYOND THE SHRUBS, THE FOAL PASSES A HUGE GRAY TRUNK AND FINALLY SEES ITS MOTHER.

THE MOTHER SEES THE FOAL. IT MOVES FORWARD BUT THEN HESITATES, CRYING OUT.

RHEEEEWHEEE

THE FOAL RUNS HEEDLESSLY ACROSS THE CLEARING TOWARD ITS MOTHER.

THE FIRST MESONYX ARRIVES AND CIRCLES AROUND THE GRAY TRUNKS, GIVING THEM A WIDE BERTH.

IT KNOWS THEY BELONG TO A UINTATHERIUM—A LARGE, KNOBBLY-FACED, RHINOLIKE CREATURE THAT IS GRAZING AT THE SWAMP'S EDGE.

BUT THE UINTATHERIUM FAMILY IS ALSO GUARDING A YOUNG ONE. AS THE MESONYX CLOSES IN ON THE EOHIPPUS MOTHER AND FOAL, THE UINTATHERIUMS' CALF CRIES OUT IN ALARM.

BWHAAA! BWHAAA!

THE MALE UINTATHERIUM TURNS TO FACE THE DANGER AND INSTINCTIVELY STAMPS ITS FRONT LEGS...

MUWHAAAA

...CRUSHING THE TAIL OF THE SECOND MESONYX AS IT CHARGES PAST.

PHSTFOMT

THE FIRST MESONYX IS NEARLY UPON THE TWO EOHIPPUSES.

GRRRRRRRR

LEAVING THE SECOND MESONYX TO **WRITHE** IN PAIN, THE UINTATHERIUM CIRCLES LIKE A BULL...

GRRRRRRRR

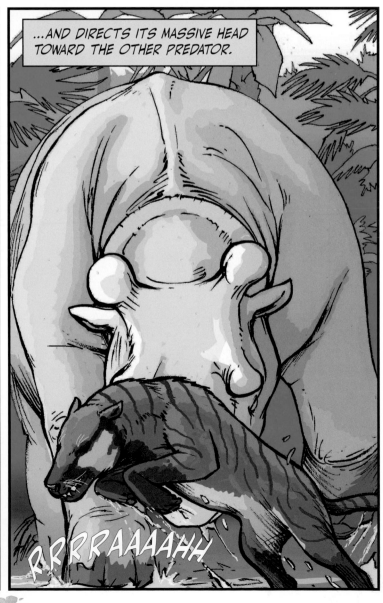

...AND DIRECTS ITS MASSIVE HEAD TOWARD THE OTHER PREDATOR.

RRRRAAAAHH

SCOOPED SKYWARD BY THE UINTATHERIUM, THE FIRST MESONYX SAILS HIGH OVER THE SWAMP...

AWOOOOOOOO

...AND LANDS MID-STREAM AMONG SOME CROCODILES.

THE HERBIVORES LUMBER AWAY, BUT THE EOHIPPUS FOAL HAS A NEW PROBLEM. IT IS NOW STUCK IN THE GLUEY MUD OF THE SWAMP EDGE.

DESPITE ITS WOUNDS, THE SECOND MESONYX EDGES MENACINGLY TOWARD THE EOHIPPUSES. IT IS DETERMINED TO MAKE A KILL.

GRRRRRR

SUDDENLY AN ENORMOUS BEAK PINS IT TO THE GROUND.

IT IS THE GASTORNIS. THE GREAT BIRD CAN'T RESIST TAKING AN EASY MEAL OF MEAT TO **SUPPLEMENT** ITS DIET.

GRRRARK!

THE FOAL FINALLY FREES ITSELF FROM THE MUD AND FLEES WITH ITS MOTHER. THEY'LL EAT WHEN THEY FIND A QUIETER, SAFER PLACE.

FOSSIL FINDS

WE CAN GET A GOOD IDEA OF WHAT **ANCIENT ANIMALS** MAY HAVE LOOKED LIKE FROM THEIR FOSSILS. FOSSILS ARE FORMED WHEN THE HARD PARTS OF AN ANIMAL OR PLANT BECOME BURIED AND THEN TURN TO ROCK OVER MILLIONS OF YEARS.

Fossils of *Eohippuses* have been found in many countries, but *Eohippuses* only evolved into horses in North America. Toward the end of the Eocene, the climate cooled. Rainforests died and were replaced by grassy plains. Even-toed ungulates had by then evolved multi-chambered stomachs to digest the rough shrubs that the hippuses (horses) and tapirs couldn't eat. This gave the ungulates an advantage. When tough grass became the main foliage, they were the major plant eaters and eventually evolved into animals such as today's pigs, goats, deer, and cattle.

The hippuses adapted too, gaining tough teeth and long legs to run fast. They also formed herds for protection. The first modern horse, the American zebra, existed 47 million years after the dawn horse.

Merychippus was the first true grazing horse and had a central toe with side toes that only touched the ground when running.

ANIMAL GALLERY

All of these **animals** appear in the story.

Shoshonius
length to tail: 12 inches (30 cm)
a small tree-dwelling **primate** that ate insects—similar to a modern-day tarsier

Smilodectes
length to tail: 16 inches (41 cm)
a small lemurlike primate that ate fruit, tree sap, and insects

Hypertragulidae
length: 24 inches (61 cm)
a small even-toed ungulate browser similar to a modern-day mousedeer

Heptodon
length: 3.3 ft (1 m)
a ground-dwelling uneven-toed ungulate browser similar to a modern-day tapir but without its trunk

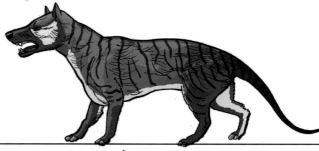

Machaeroides
"daggerlike"
length: 5–6.5 ft (1.5–2 m)
a catlike meat eater; the first-ever sabertoothed mammal discovered

Mesonyx
"middle claw"
length: 5 ft (1.5 m)
a wolflike predator with hooves on its toes, instead of claws, and a powerful bite

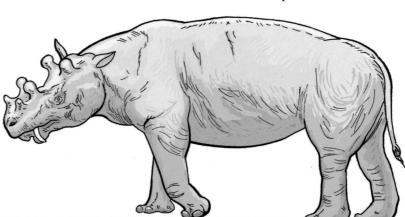

Gastornis
(named after its discoverer Gaston Planté)
height: up to 6.6 ft (2 m)
a tall, heavily-built flightless bird with a massive beak that probably fed on fruits and seeds

Uintatherium
"beast of the Uinta Mountains"
length: 13 ft (4 m)
a rhino-sized browser with a hard-boned knobbly head, fangs, and a small brain for its size

GLOSSARY

browser an animal that eats mainly leaves, twigs, and nuts

Eocene period a time between 56,000,000 to 33,900,000 years ago when Earth's land was entirely covered by jungle

fibrous tough, woody

fossil the remains of living things that have turned to rock

instinctively doing something without thinking

primate a mammmal with forward-looking eyes and five-fingered hands and feet that lives in trees (except for humans)

sabertooth a sharp, extra-long, meat-tearing tooth

secluded sheltered, private

supplement an extra foodstuff that improves diet

tentatively fearfully and uncertainly

ungulate an animal with toes that end in hooves, not claws

writhe to twist and turn the body due to pain

INDEX